HOLIDAYS AND FESTIVALS

Christmas

Nancy Dickmann

Heinemann Library
Chicago, Illinois

www.capstonepub.com
Visit our website to find out
more information about
Heinemann-Raintree books.

To order:

☎ Phone 800-747-4992
💻 Visit www.capstonepub.com
to browse our catalog and order online.

©2011 Heinemann Library
an imprint of Capstone Global Library, LLC
Chicago, Illinois

Edited by Sian Smith, Nancy Dickmann, and Rebecca Rissman
Designed by Steve Mead
Picture research by Elizabeth Alexander
Production by Victoria Fitzgerald
Originated by Capstone Global Library Ltd
Printed and bound in the United States of America in
North Mankato, Minnesota. 012016 009378RP

The content consultant was Richard Aubrey. Richard is a teacher of Religious
Education with a particular interest in Philosophy for Children.

17 16 15
10 9 8 7 6 5

Library of Congress Cataloging-in-Publication Data
Dickmann, Nancy.
  Christmas / Nancy Dickmann.
    p. cm.—(Holidays and Festivals)
  Includes bibliographical references and index.
  ISBN 978-1-4329-4047-8 (hc)—ISBN 978-1-4329-4066-9 (pb)
  1. Christmas—Juvenile literature. I. Title.
  BV45.D53 2011
    394.2663—dc22
                                        2009054303

Acknowledgments
We would like to thank the following for permission to reproduce
photographs: Alamy pp. **5** (© i love images), **8** (© World Religions Photo
Library), **9** (© LHB Photo), **12**, **20** (© Image Source), **15**, **23 top** (© Adrian
Sherratt), **21** (© Frances Roberts), **23 bottom** (© World Religions Photo
Library); Corbis pp. **6** (© The Gallery Collection), **7** (© Lebrecht Music
& Arts), **19** (© Larry Williams); Getty Images pp. **4** (Thinkstock), **10**, **23
middle** (Yellow Dog Productions/The Image Bank), **11** (Cameron Spencer),
13 (Romeo Gacad/AFP), **16** (Peter Dazeley/Photodisc), **18** (Heinrich van
den Berg); On Asia Images p. **14** (Lu Guang); Shutterstock pp. **17** (©
Monkey Business Images), **22 top left** (© bhathaway), **22 top right** (©
Doremi), **22 bottom left** (© Jurand), **bottom right** (© carballo).

Front cover photograph of nativity scene reproduced with permission of
iStockphoto (© Lisa Thornberg). Back cover photograph reproduced with
permission of Alamy (© Adrian Sherratt).

We would like to thank Diana Bentley, Dee Reid, Nancy Harris, and
Richard Aubrey for their invaluable help in the preparation of this book.

Every effort has been made to contact copyright holders of any material
reproduced in this book. Any omissions will be rectified in subsequent
printings if notice is given to the publisher.

Contents

What Is a Festival?

A festival is a time when people come together to celebrate.

Christian people celebrate Christmas on the 25th of December.

The Story of Christmas

Jesus

Long ago, a baby called Jesus was born.

Jesus's parents had nowhere
to stay.

Jesus was born in a stable.

Christian people believe he was the
son of God.

Celebrating Christmas Today

Christmas is when Christian people celebrate Jesus's birthday.

People celebrate Christmas in different ways.

Some people put up decorations.

Some people have a Christmas tree.

Some people go to church.

Some people sing carols.

Some people send cards.

Some people get together and eat a special meal.

Some people give gifts.

Santa Claus

Some people believe Santa Claus brings them gifts.

Christmas is a time for kindness.

Christmas is a time for giving to others.

Look and See

Christmas tree

Santa Claus

Jesus

star

Have you seen these things? They make people think of Christmas.

Picture Glossary

 **carol** special song that is sung at festivals

 **Christian people** people who follow the teachings of Jesus

 **stable** building where animals live

23

Index

Note to Parents and Teachers

Before reading

Ask the children if they know what holidays and festivals are. Can they name any festivals they celebrate with their families? Talk about birthdays and why they are celebrated. How do they ce their own birthday? Christian people, who follow the religion of Christianity celebrate the birth of Je at Christmas. Some children from non-Christian or non-religious families may also celebrate Christmas in a secular way.

After reading

• Provide a selection of Christmas cards, both religious and secular. Ask the children to look at the symbols and decorations used. Which aspects of Christmas do they think each one represents? Help the children to design their own Christmas cards.

• Explain that Advent is the period of preparation for the celebration of the birth of Jesus and lasts for about four weeks. The name comes from the Latin 'adventus' which means 'coming'. Talk about ways people celebrate Advent, such as by lighting candles or keeping Advent calendars. Help the children to make an Advent wreath.

• Discuss the idea that some of the most appreciated gifts are not objects but gifts of time and love. Ask the children to think of 'invisible gifts' for their family and friends. Suggest ideas such as sharing a favorite toy, helping out with household chores, or doing a favorite activity together. Help the children make personalized 'gift vouchers' to give to family and friends.

24